Draw with . . .

Joan Miró

"I'm not interested in a painting that just stays on the wall. What excites me is its radiance, its message, and what it can do to transform people's minds in some small way."

Joan Miró

F

FRANCES LINCOLN
CHILDREN'S BOOKS

www.franceslincoln.com

Miró in Paris
in 1957

THE POETRY OF JOAN MIRÓ

Enter a fantastical new world!

Miró's paintings often look naïve and childlike. In order to show his imaginary world in painting he had to create his own language in pictures. The simple shapes he used resembled those of children's drawings.

"I am in my cave, like a child in its cave."

Joan Miró was born in 1893 in Catalonia, Spain, and showed a remarkable artistic talent from a very early age. His parents would be astonished by his dedication and focus as he sat drawing with his coloured pencils for hours at a time.

By 1907 he was studying at both the Barcelona Business School and at the Fine Arts Academy in Lonja, and in 1920 Miró moved to Paris in France. He was astounded by the beauty of the city and was inspired by his experiences there: meeting the artist Pablo Picasso, attending demonstrations by people supporting the Dada movement, and visiting the Louvre Museum.

In 1923, heavily influenced by the ideas of another artistic group called

*Ladders Cross the Blue Sky
in a Wheel of Fire, 1953*

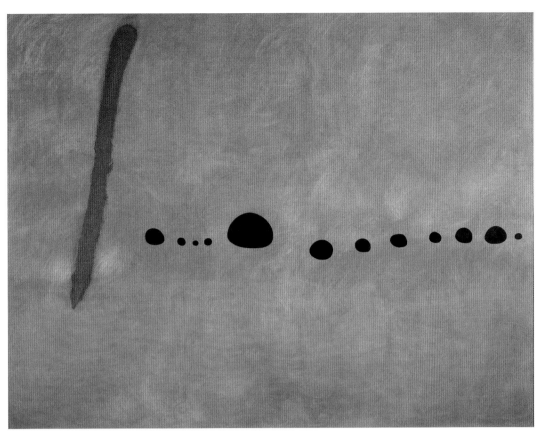

Blue II, 4 March 1961

the Surrealists, Miró began to draw on his dreams as subject matter for his paintings. He never completely abandoned realistic representation, but he was now attempting to

Coloured woodcut for Paul Eluard's *À toute épreuve (Steadfast),* 1958

incorporate symbols and imaginary elements into his work.

In 1937 he began work on what became his famous *Constellations* series. These paintings were scattered with images of stars, moons and suns, as well as eyes and fantastical shapes inspired by music and nature.

After World War II, Miró's paintings became simpler and more meditative. His famous *Blue* triptych is a good example of the new style, but he was still trying to do the same thing: find a way of expressing a childlike innocence and the creative magic of an infant's first scribblings.

"These three great blue canvases . . . are the culmination of everything I have been trying to do all my life."

He continued to work right up till his death on Christmas Day 1983. He was ninety years old.

SKY

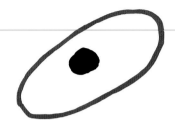

1

2

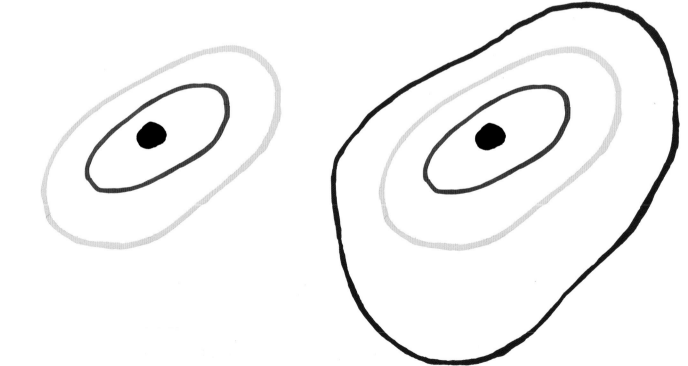

3

4

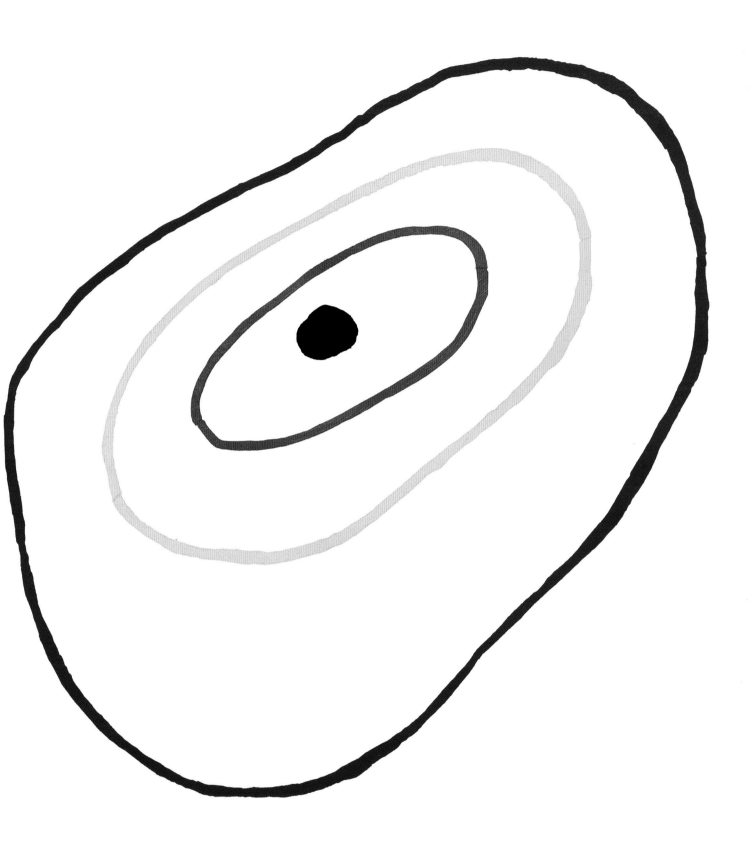

"In many of my paintings you can see spheres and circles,
which are the evocation of the ruling planets."

1

2

"The spectacle of the sky overwhelms me."

3

4

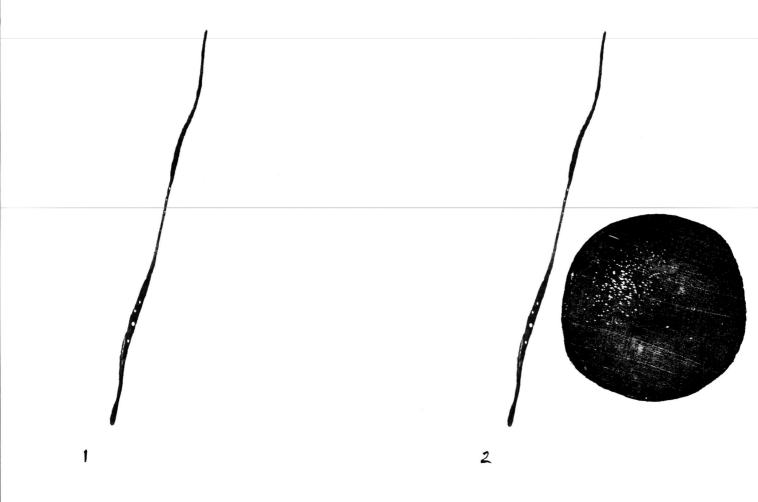

1

2

"That splash of colour is the most authentic thing.
It's from there that my journey can begin."

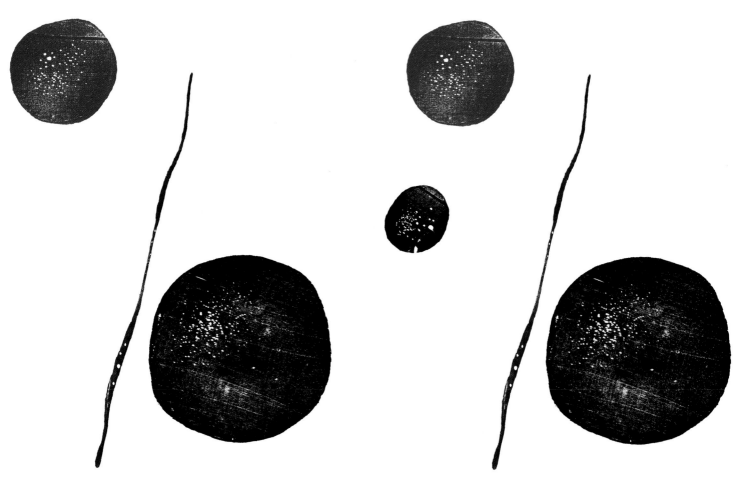

3

4

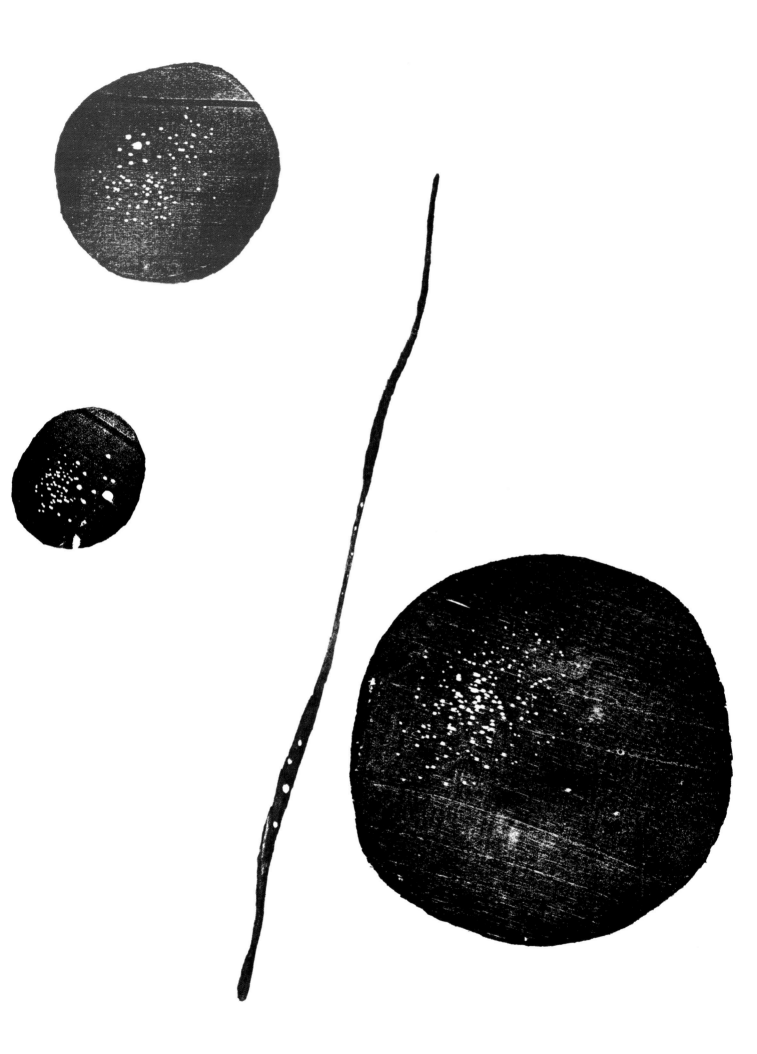

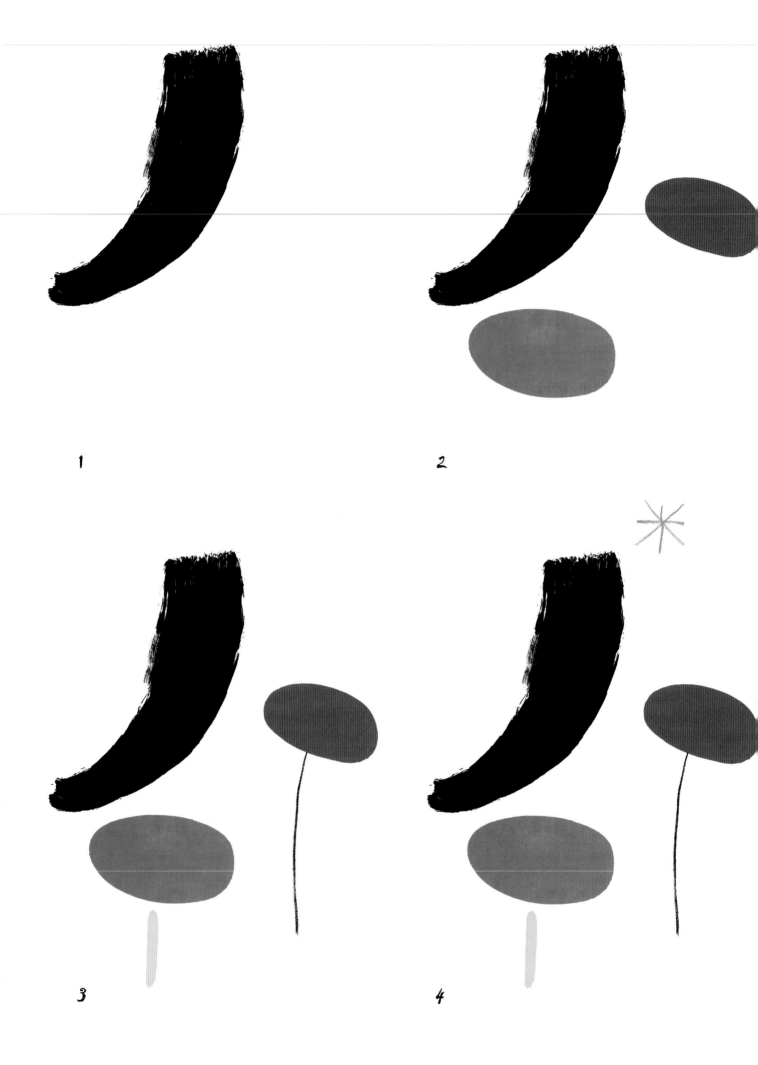

1

2

3

4

"I am stunned when I see a tree. It's as though it breathes, as though it talks."

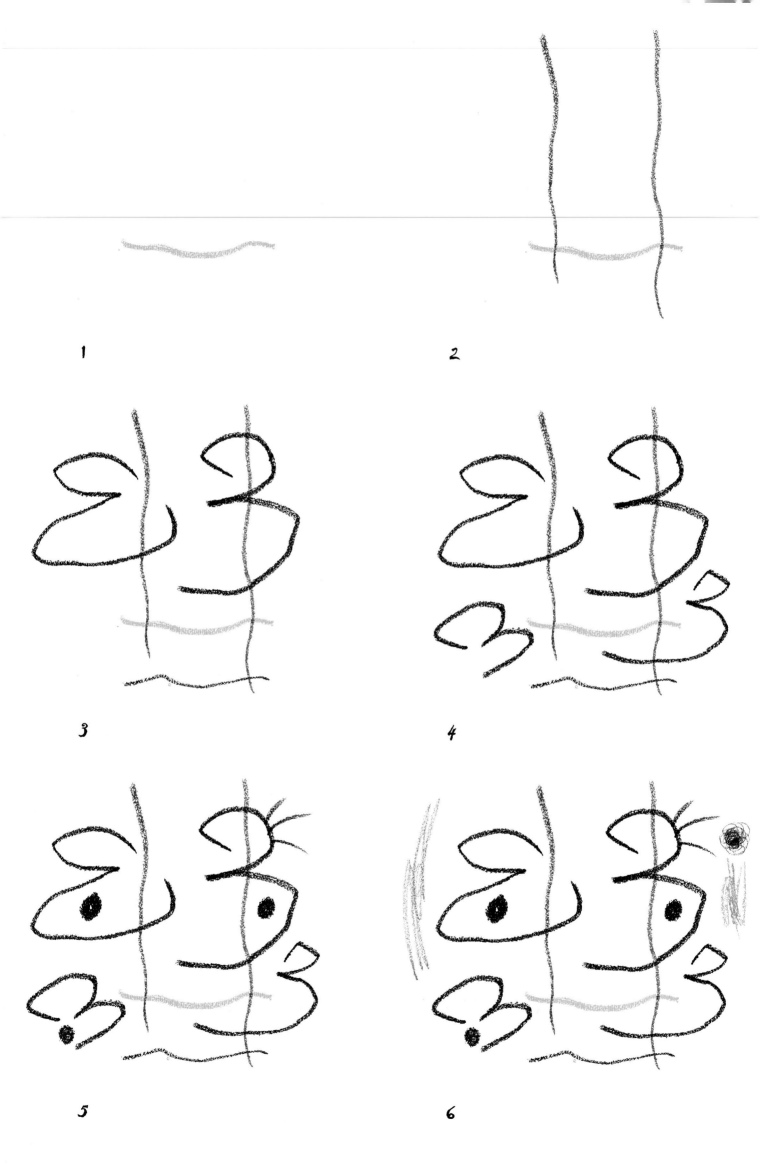

1

2

3

4

5

6

"My painting is more and more about making gestures."

CONSTELLATIONS

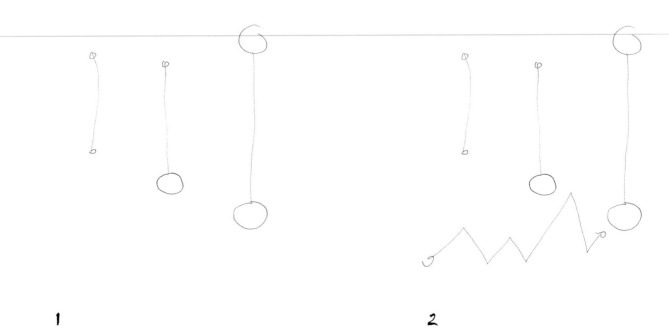

1

2

"The painting looks back at me like an arrow."

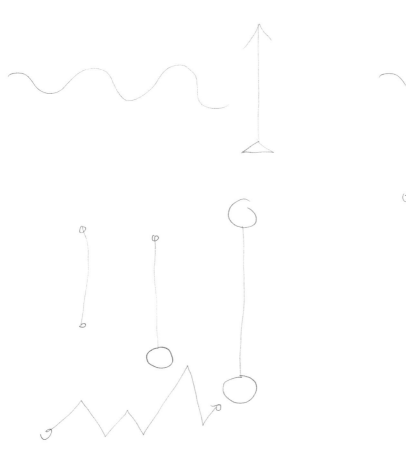

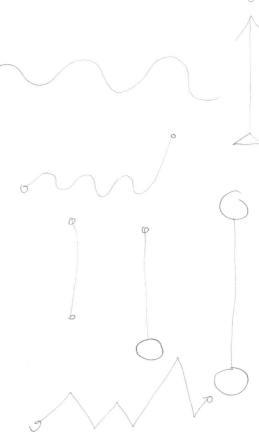

3

4

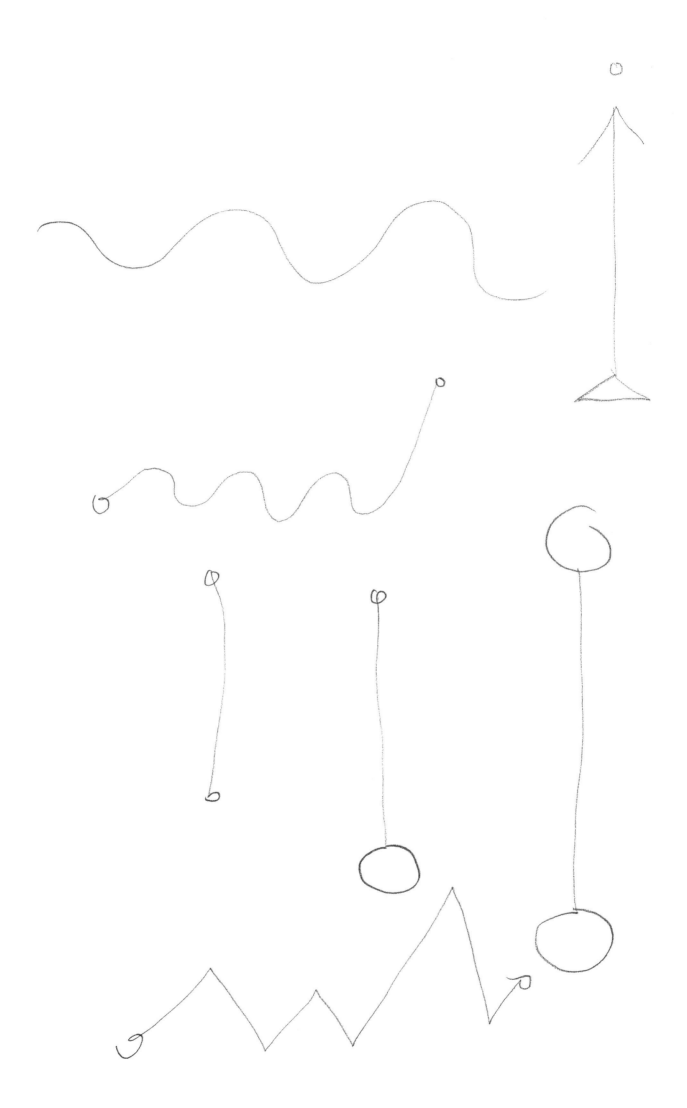

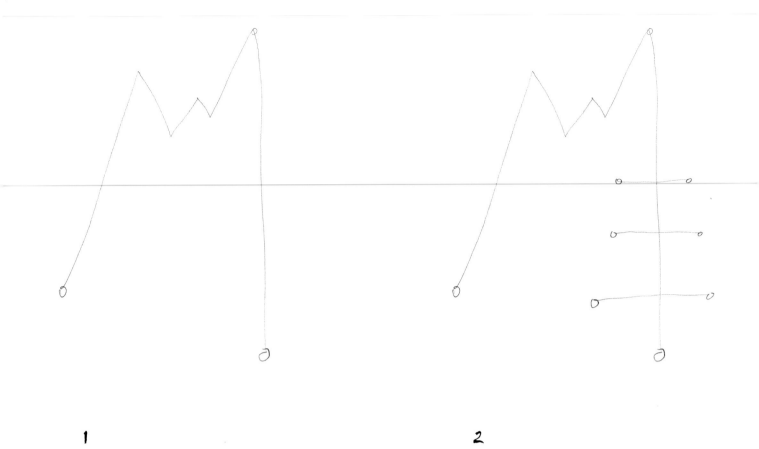

1

2

"In art the only thing that counts is that magical spark."

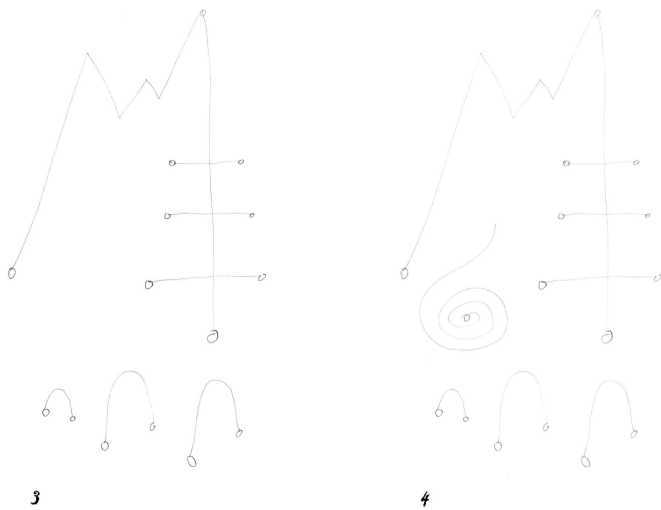

3

4

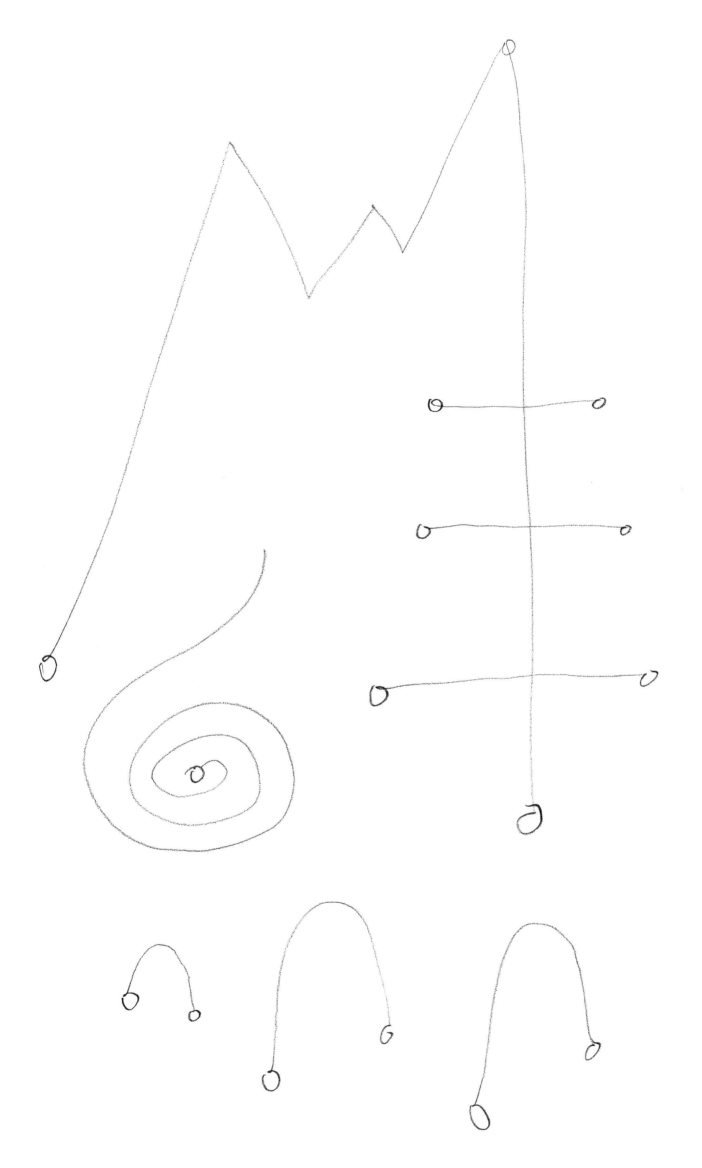

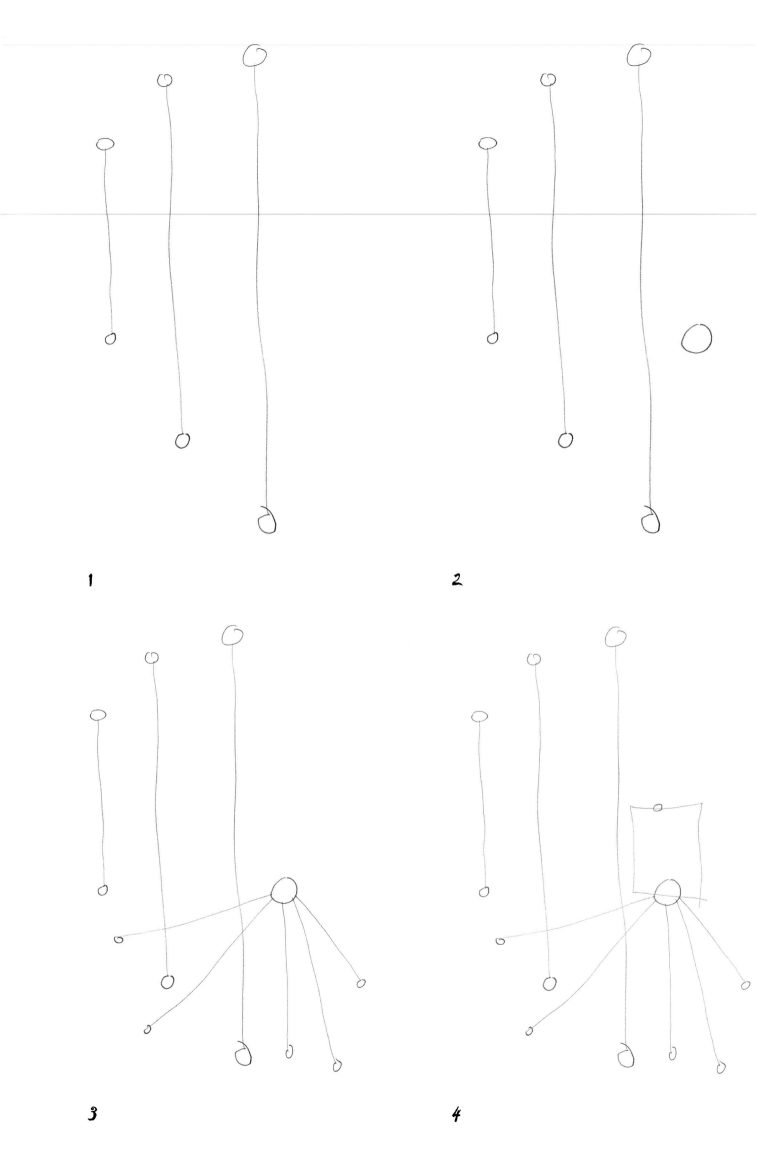

1

2

3

4

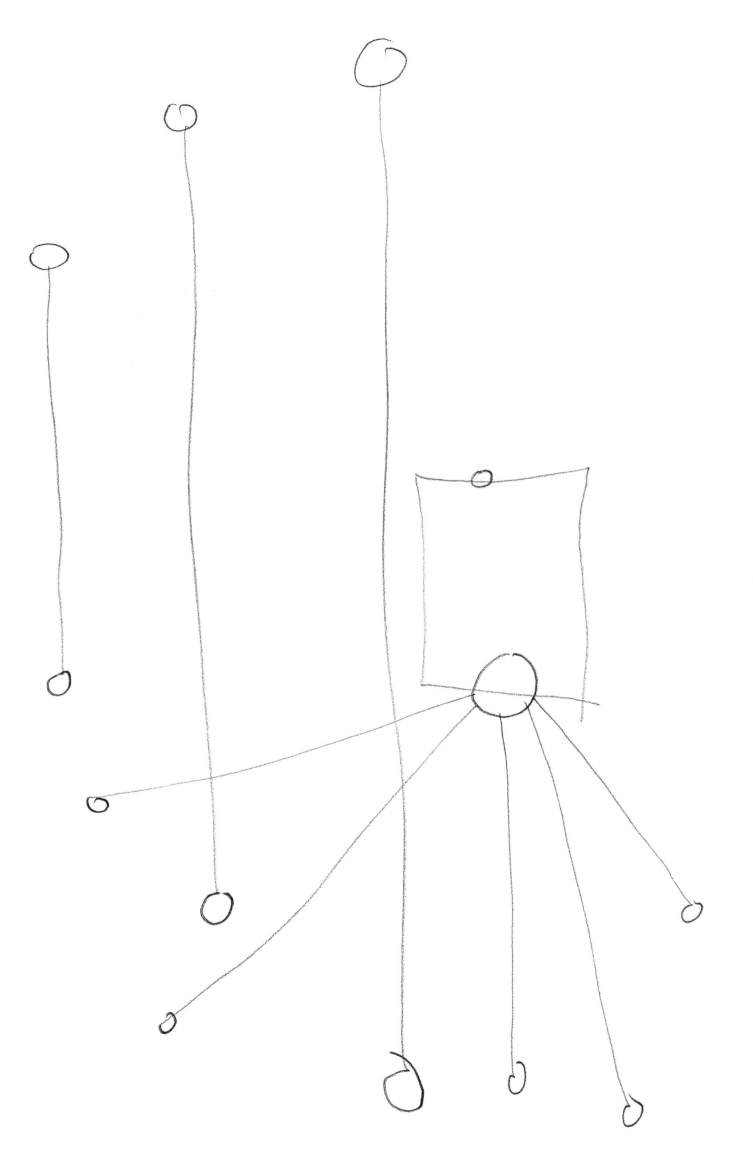

BIRDS

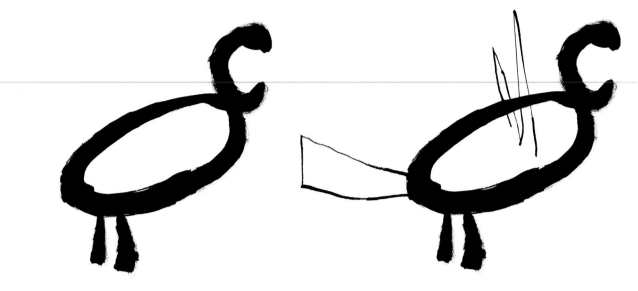

1

2

"I marvel at a little bird that can fly."

3

4

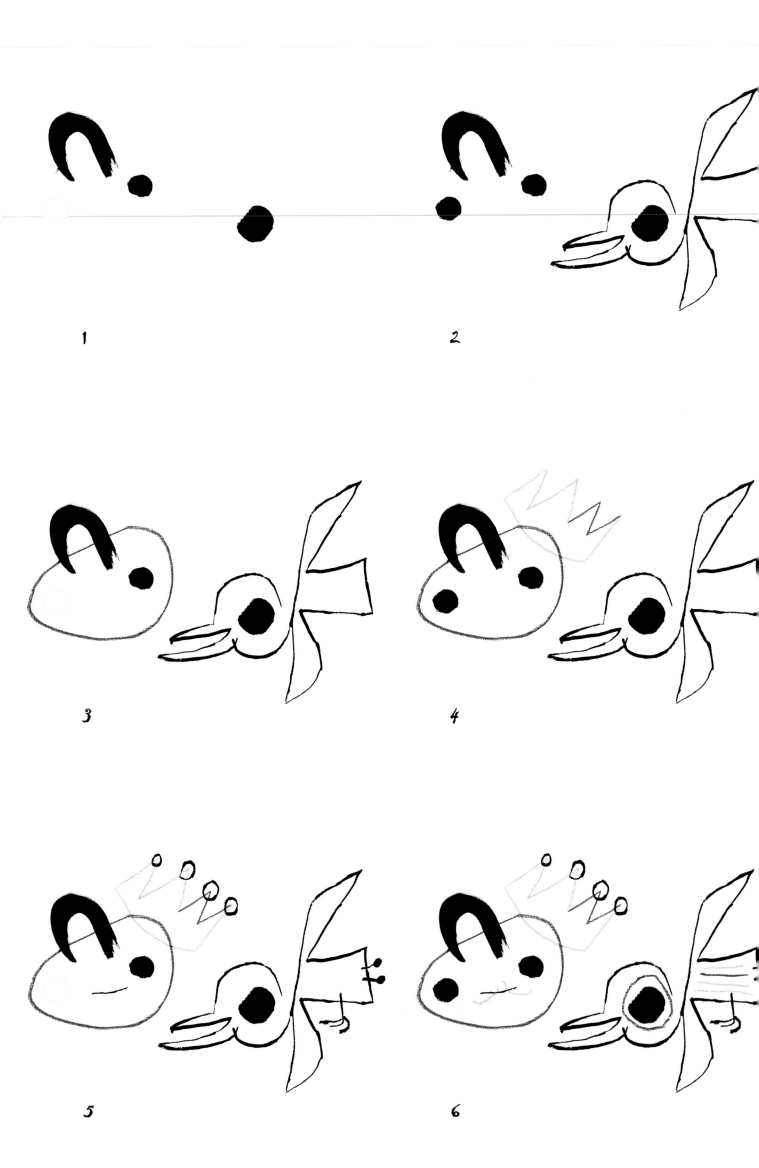

1

2

3

4

5

6

"A shape gives me an idea. That idea gives rise to
another shape, and all these elements end up as figures,
or animals, or even things I don't recognise
and never imagined."

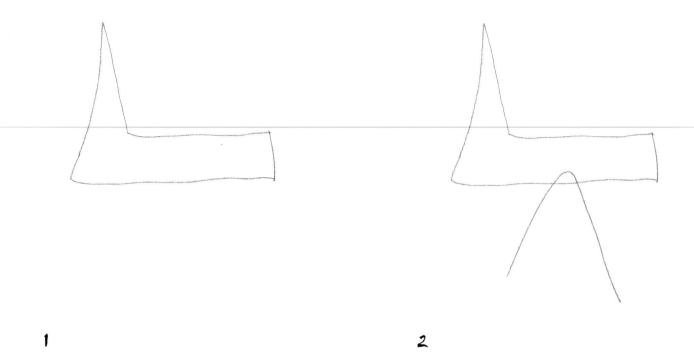

1

2

"When I have an idea, I make a little sketch of it wherever I am, on whatever I've got to hand. As time passes the idea works away at the back of my mind, and one day it becomes a painting."

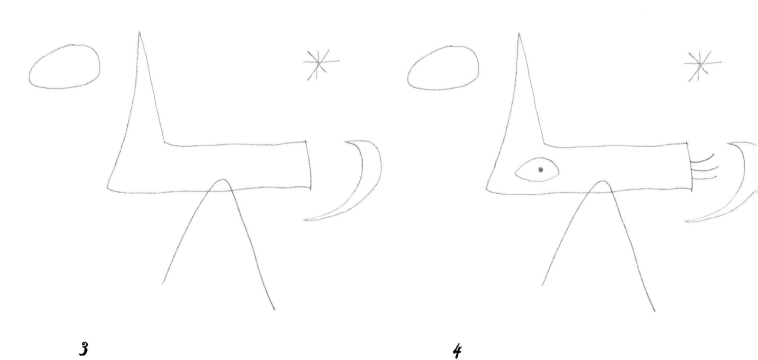

3

4

1

2

3

4

5

6

FIGURES

1

2

3

4

"Every time you look at a painting you should be able to see something new in it."

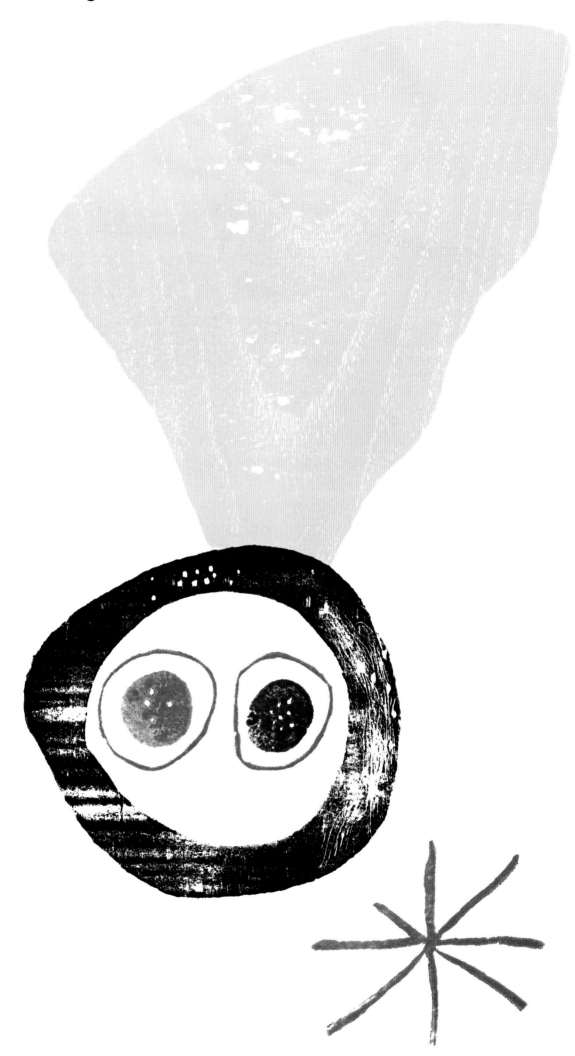

1

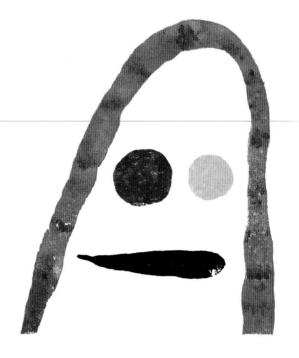

2

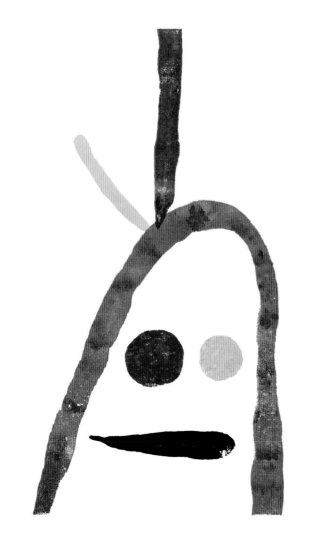

3

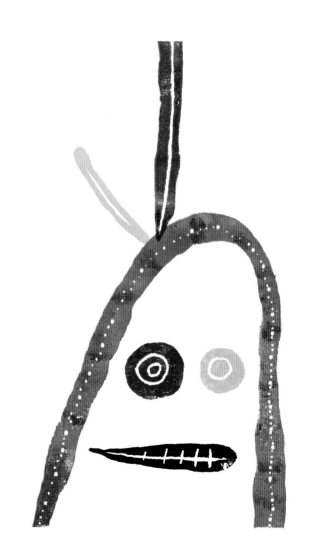

4

1

2

3

4

5

6

"You must not crush the vitality of the living line –
it is like a beating heart."

1

2

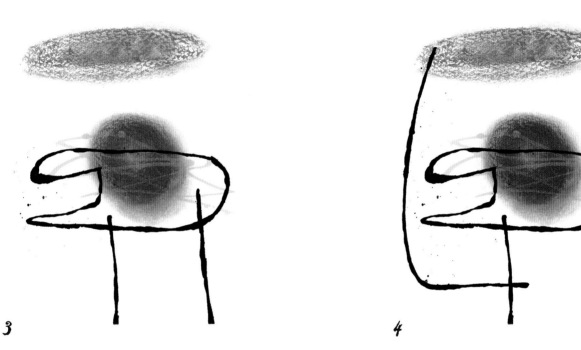

3

4

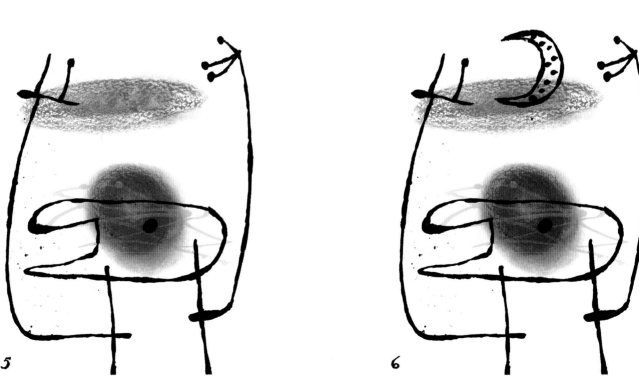

5

6

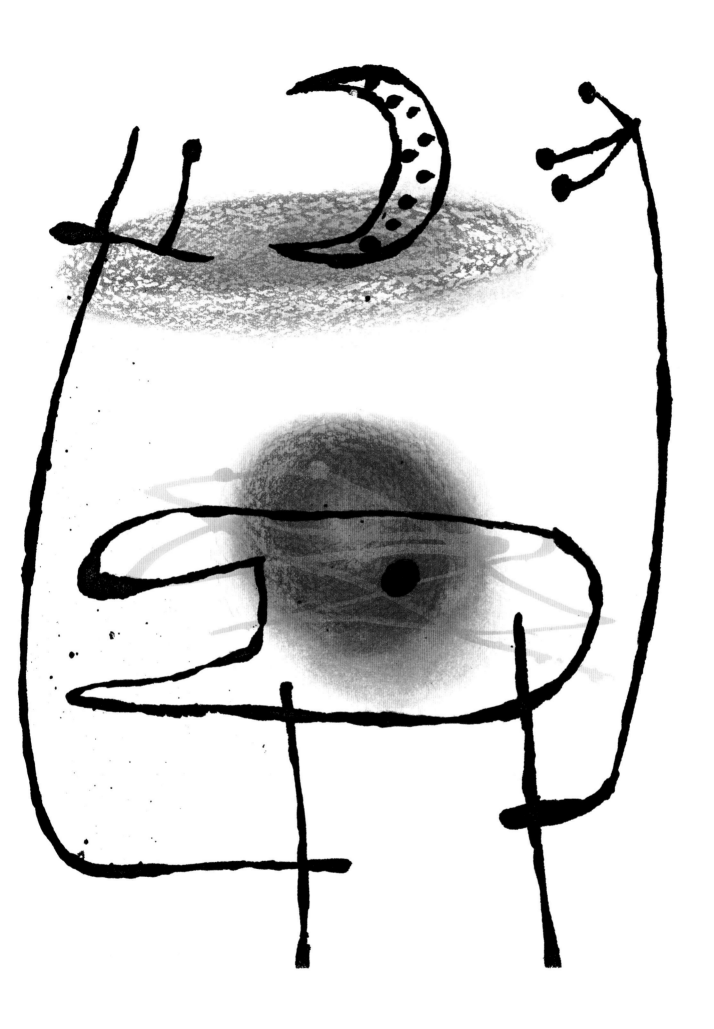

"When I am working, when I am awake – it's then that I dream."

1

2

3

4

5

6

"A work is finished when there is nothing left that annoys me."

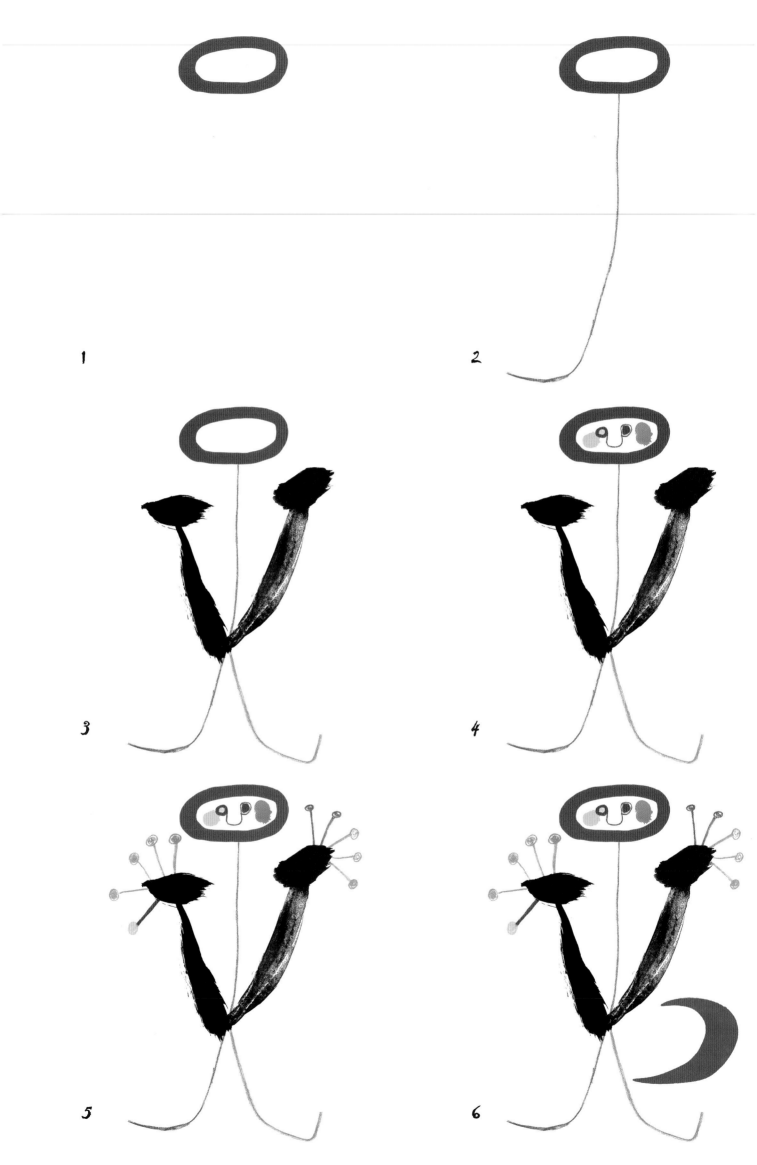

1

2

3

4

5

6

"Treat figures like plants and flowers – with extreme simplicity and poetry."

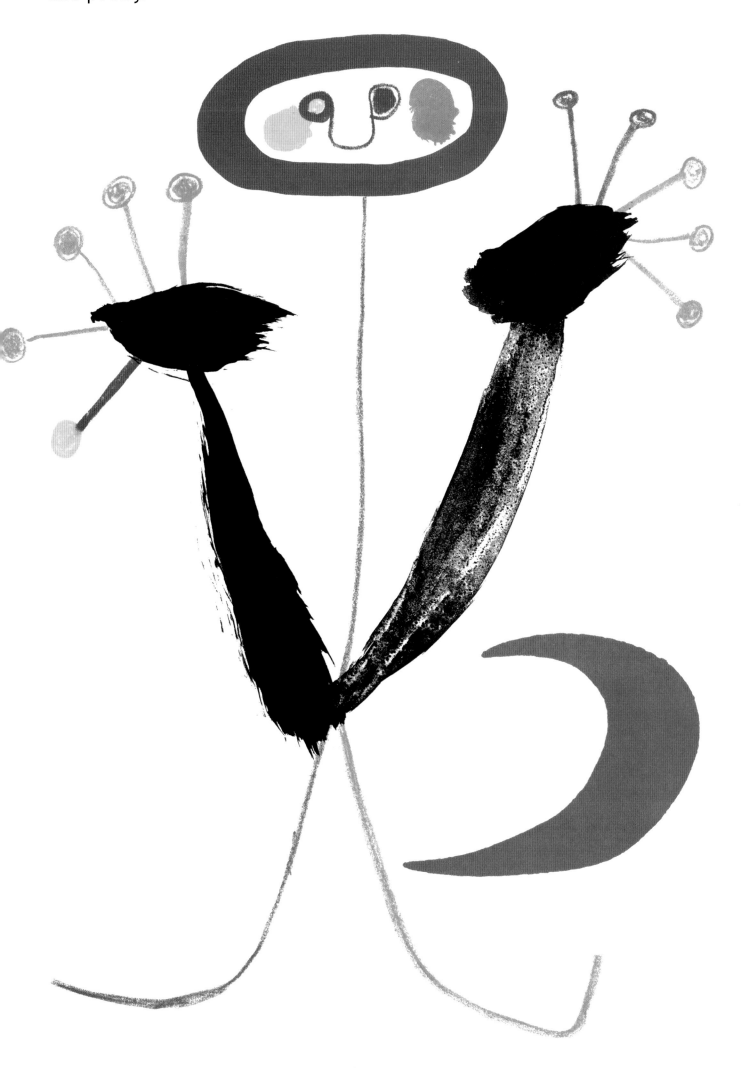

1

2

3

4

5

6

1

2

3

4

5

6

"The figures are more human and more alive
than if I showed them in all their detail."

1

2

3

4

"If I don't work, I lose my equilibrium."

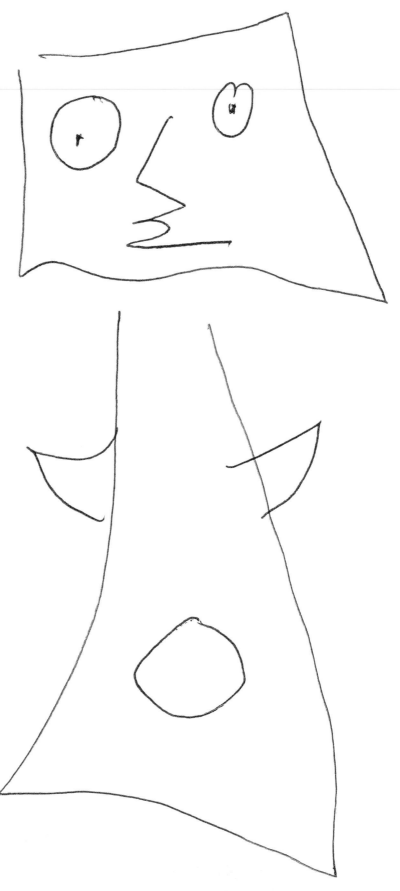

"In sculpture I shall create a truly fantasmagorical world."

PICTURE CREDITS

Untitled, coloured lithographs for *Parler Seul (Talking Alone)* by Tristan Tzara, 1948-1950, Maeght Éditeur, Paris. Photograph © French National Library, Paris.

  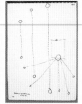 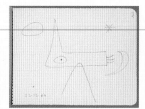  

Sketches for *Composicio (Composition)*, pencil on paper, Joan Miró Foundation, Barcelona. Foundation's own photograph.

1941, 33.8 x 24.6 cm   1941, 33.8 x 24.6 cm   1941, 33.8 x 24.6 cm   1944, 16 x 21 cm   1944, 31.5 x 22 cm

Aquatints, 14 x 11.5 cm, for *La bague d'Aurore (The Ring of Dawn)* by René Crevel, 1957, Éditions Louise Brodeur, Paris

Photograph © Joan Miró Foundation, Barcelona

Photograph © French National Library, Paris

Drawings for *Ubu Roi (King Ubu)* 1970, Chinese ink, wax crayon and pencil on paper, 32.7 x 50.2 cm, Joan Miró Foundation, Barcelona. Foundation's own photograph.

Coloured woodcuts for *À toute épreuve (Steadfast)* by Paul Eluard, 1958, Éditions Gérald Cramer, Geneva. Photograph © French National Library, Paris.

 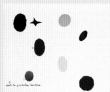

Coloured stencil prints for *Il était une petite pie (There Was a Little Magpie)* by Lise Hirtz, 1928, Éditions Jeanne Bucher, Paris. Photograph © French National Library, Paris.

n° I   n° IV

Coloured lithograph, approximately 64 x 48.5 cm, for *Album 21* by Carlos Franqui, 1978, Maeght Éditeur, Paris, Photograph © French National Library, Paris.

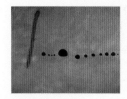

Blue II, 4 March 1961, oil on canvas, 270 x 355 cm, Georges Pompidou Centre National Museum of Modern Art, Paris. Photograph © Philippe Migeat/CNAC/MNAM Dist./RMN.

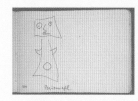

Preparatory drawing for *Personatge (Figure)*, 1973, pen on paper, 21.2 x 31 cm, Joan Miró Foundation, Barcelona. Foundation's own photograph.

Personatge (Figure), 1973, bronze, 70 x 32.5 x 12 cm, Joan Miró Foundation, Barcelona. Foundation's own photograph.

Les échelles en roue de feu traversent l'azur (Ladders Cross the Blue Sky in a Wheel of Fire), 1953, oil on canvas, 116 x 89 cm, private collection. Photograph © Bridgeman-Giraudon.

Miró in the Crommelynck brothers' studio, Boulevard des Invalides, Paris, 1957. Photograph © Michel Sima/Rue des Archives.

Preparatory drawing for *Pintura (Painting)*, 1930, pencil on paper, 19.1 x 13.1 cm, Joan Miró Foundation, Barcelona. Foundation's own photograph.

BIBLIOGRAPHY

Miró, le peintre aux étoiles (Miró, the Star-Painter) by Joan Punyet Miró and Gloria Lolivier-Rahola, Découvertes Gallimard, 1993
Quotations selected by Yvon Taillandier from *xx siècle (20th Century)*, vol. I, no. 1, Paris, February 1959
Miró, ceci est la couleur de mes rêves (Miró: The Colour of my Dreams), interviews with Georges Raillard, Éditions du Seuil, 2004
Joan Miró, écrits et entretiens (Miró: Writings and Interviews) edited by Margrit Rowell, Daniel Lelong Éditeur, 1995

Text and illustrations copyright © Gallimard Jeunesse 2007   First published under the title *Dessiner avec . . . Joan Miró* by Gallimard Jeunesse, Paris, France   First published in Great Britain and the USA in 2011 by Frances Lincoln Children's Books, 4 Torriano Mews, Torriano Avenue, London NW5 2RZ   www.franceslincoln.com
Text by Ana Salvador   English translation © Antonia Parkin 2011   All rights reserved   A catalogue record is available from the British Library
ISBN: 978-1-84780-272-9   Printed in Dongguan, Guangdong, China by Toppan Leefung in January 2011   9 8 7 6 5 4 3 2 1